T4-AIL-991

APPEARING BY DAYLIGHT

David Sten Herrstrom

Drawings by Jacob Landau

Grateful acknowledgement is made
to the editor of AMBROSIA PRESS
who published *Jonah's Disappearance*
and to the editors of the following periodicals
in which these poems previously appeared:

SOURCE: "Mary Magdalene"; "The Fish Sermon"

THE THIRD WIND: "Five Hundred Witness"; "Tall Walking
Figure"

US1 WORKSHEETS: "What Thomas Said."

* * * *

Earlier versions of my stories can be found in the Bible:

Jonah ("Jonah's Disappearance")
John 11:1-44 ("Inventions of Lazarus")
John 20:11-18 ("Mary Magdalene in the Garden")
John 21 ("The Fish Sermon")
Matthew 28:16-18 and I Corinthians 15:6 ("Five Hundred
    Witness")
Luke 24:13-31 ("Tall Walking Figure")
John 20:26-28 ("What Thomas Said")

I have also taken some of Jesus' words from the Gospel of
Thomas, found at Nag Hammadi, and with gratitude ransacked
the stories of many other writers, from Blake to Toby Olson; for
stories beget stories.

AEGINA PRESS, Inc.
59 Oak Lane, Spring Valley
Huntington, West Virginia 25704

CONTENTS

The mother part of this book for
N. Hazel Stratford Herrstrom

The father part for
S. Gunnar Herrstrom

APPEARING BY DAYLIGHT

In the eyes of God, who cuts
through appearances and goes beyond
them, there is no art, for art
thrives on appearances.
                                —Sartre

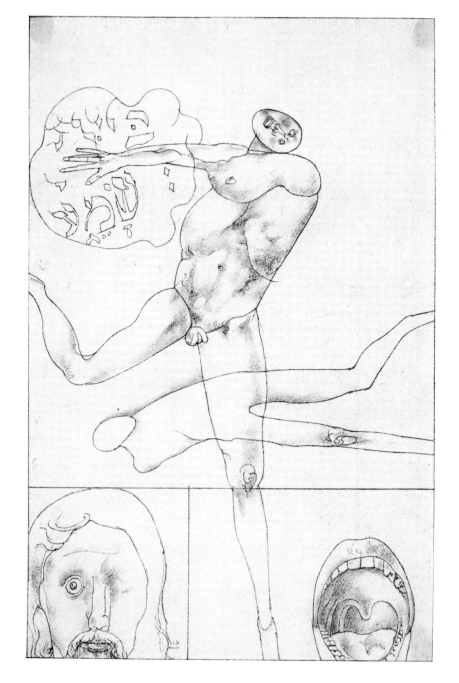

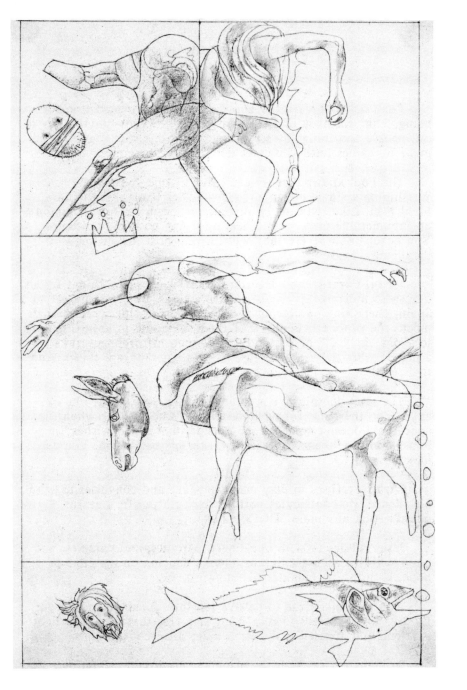

Prologue

#

The Fool, like curiosity and desire, has his own reason for being. This is a book of Fools, whose way to know anything is to call people and things by silly names until one sticks, and to make up games until you can't tell if you're playing or not.

The Fool knows that we can't live by one god alone. Worshiping a single metaphor is death. For Fools there is no Final Fact. Like shamans in all times everywhere, they summon up innumerable presences to heal by trying on many costumes. You never know where they will turn up next, never know if they'll stay dead.

Jonah, Lazarus, and Jesus are Fools. They name things for us otherwise unnamed, by irresponsible actions, like running off to Spain, cherishing outrageous silences, or proffering words. Jonah mocks the prophets, Fools all of them, by going to absurd lengths to avoid his "call" or wishing to die when his prophecy fails for a people who, precisely because they're ignorant, are saved. And their cattle.

The Fool doesn't give a damn for what saves, but, like anyone on the road, for what sustains. It's no wonder when the apocalypse doesn't come on the outside, that Jonah wishes "in himself to die," because dead he writes his best poem. You can look it up.

Lazarus refuses to play magus or guru and convulses us with his silence. He contributes nothing in death to life. Lazarus doesn't stink any more. That's enough.

Jesus riddles us with one-liners, parodies, and parables, and plays with his accusers like us, always dancing on the edge of hope, brandishing laughter like a sword.

And they all refuse to behave sensibly. Jonah refuses to go; Lazarus to talk; Jesus to rule. They stay free that way. The Fool is friend and accuser at the same time, different costumes.

So their quarrel with the original *Appearing by Daylight*, commonly known as the *Egyptian Book of the Dead*, Baedeker to the land beyond. They're not about to toady to death, claim good behavior, and buy a villa in that land. None thrilled with the Afterlife. All stayed only three days, evidently preferring bodies to souls, one world to two.

Besides, guide books are too sensible. That's why none of them wrote a word, to say nothing of their exasperating insistence on coming back. And after they returned from darkness, games seemed not only a good idea but necessary. All were appalled to discover that the mystic and the materialist are literal-minded brothers. Neither thinks sex is funny.

It's the old problem of Desire. Anyone who can do without it is not a Fool. But playing for high stakes makes you nervous. Jonah feared the consequences of power; Lazarus those of knowledge; Jesus of desire. Yet they all gambled on the vulgar, the incomplete, the anarchic.

#

Reading this book you'll discover the canary's beak in the squid, who is an improbable, dangerous creature with too thick a name anyway. Remember Korf's new kind of joke, the point comes days, even years later. One night it wakes you, holding your sides and howling. So loud, you disturb poets in Mexico, like Octavio Paz who names this unreasonable, welcome fit the laughter that "restores the universe to its original state of indifference and strangeness." Or you may emerge from these poems to find yourself in brittle light on a hill overlooking the Pacific, the aroma of eucalyptus trees riding the heat beside you.

#

Think of a comic book with its framed scenes, melodrama, violence, and bubbles of talk. Who can take Jonah seriously? The funniest and yet most formal story in that great anthology is the Book of Jonah.

Name the most disappointing story in western literature. Right, that of Lazarus, who returns from the dead without a tale. Unforgivable. And Jesus, whose stories anger the elders and stump his disciples, preaches love on the Mount, but later in an interview claims to bring the sword not peace.

But we have to admire the self-pitying coward with the guts to patronize God himself; the polite lad who steps out of death as if it were a limo; and the strident Galilean who rides his ass into Jerusalem—meaning the end of Rome—and pretends he's a Fool like Jonah.

Why has western literature elevated Job, that great stay-at-home and his book of tragic tableaus, when these picaresques of

9

desire abound in petulance, cheek, and incredulity? Constantly on the move, they live seriously within frames no one can take seriously, like kids on a playground.

These poems too won't stand still. They touch on the biblical versions like a stone skipping across the lake in a game of Ducks & Drakes. A play on the canon, an addition to it, and, of course, the stone sinks in the end. Make what you want of that, applesauce or apocalypse—yucka, yucka, yucka, that's all folks.

#

Walking a path between two buildings on an ordinary October day, just before I reach some stone steps rising, I am gorged with gratitude. A preposterous, yearning gratitude completely without object or direction seizes me. The world intrudes unreasonably like an ache. Fall leaves flame to the ground. The light fits my body. The pavement flexes my leg. I feel the presence of the elm beside me and the knowledge that the cat at the top of the stairs possesses of my own presence. I cannot move for the throttling silent laughter that this one world of precise, feeling parts should be, rather than not be.

And on an ordinary October day five years later my mother dies. I remember her painting my portrait in this month on my birthday, when to sit still was unnatural. She is carried to a crematory, while in the California orchards, they gather the twigs from pruning into great heaps and burn them. Not the first time a mother dead in October, but the first for me. Again, I cannot move, as if suspended in a charged field—that she should not be, rather than be.

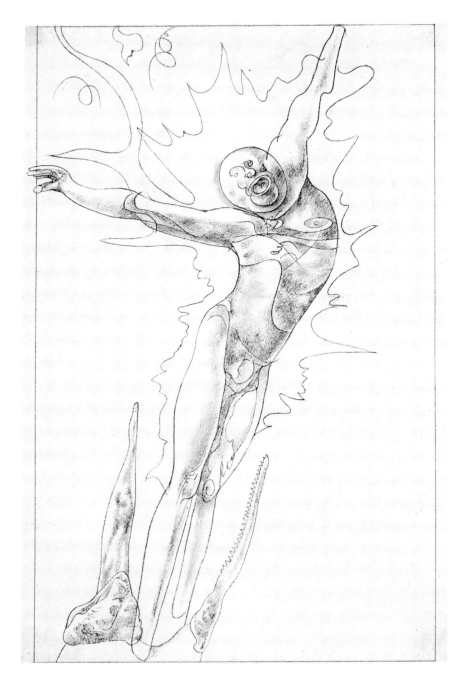

JONAH'S DISAPPEARANCE

His Call

'O Sleeper'

His Dive

His Song

His Fear

His Faint

His Anger

*

And did not Jonah resist once?
Out of the blackness
        of darkness in the belly
        of Death make a song?
Was the poet Jonah petulant and
did he sit in self-pity?
        Was Jonah angry
or did he wish for death?

*

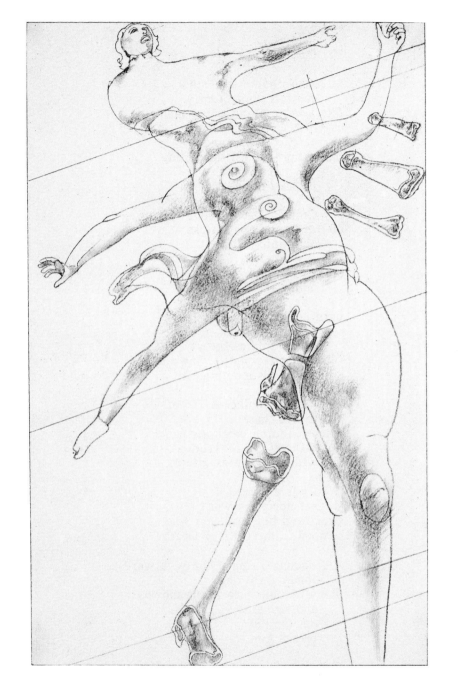

His Call

In Jonah's house the father
      controls the words,
Every morning he leaves them
caged in an empty room
      perched all around
their songs against the ceiling
        green feathers
      just out of reach.

      Crouched at the edge
of the desert Jonah tricks
      quail into calling.

He sits in the low fog in—
      haling their whistles.
      They prod his ribs
until he knows himself
      half woman
      grows bold as speech
      characters multiplying and
      out of his mouth a city.

And he left mother & father
      to live there
where children mock his name
      —Dove, son of Truth—
      with their whiny minors:

'Who was drowned
      yet never got wet
swallowed but not eaten who
camped in the belly of Death?'

A schoolmate stones him with words.
      Jonah grabs one
like a foxhole hero in the movies
      and strikes
      out the kid
      breaks him.

Expelling for fighting, Jonah
carries a storm in his belly
      home can't shake
      his own name or
      tell his father.
For three days he sleeps.

Returned to desert
the city bloomed from his gums
only remembered

he avoids the quail.
Their clean call
glints in the sand at his feet
like an ax head
and he cries out
fleeing to a friend's.
When he opens his mouth
words thud on the floor not
like frogs or coins
but heavy as houses.

'O Sleeper'

A 'fugitive'
    everyone says it
    but the 'slouched hat
and guilty eye' pure Hollywood.
    On the wharf
skulking when the captain comes
    you plunk down coins
    for passage to Spain.

They lap the sail line snug
    till it sings
    gather in the guides.
The great sail falls.
Winds welter the gray water
twist together, crash.

Jonah lies in a sleep
    deep as mud.
The ship bowels rumble
popping like champagne corks.
Jonah sounder than Adam
    dreaming the rib
that rises & beckons
    and those names
    crowding him.

The Helmsman
    with Ahab's foot
shoves him & shouts, 'Stand!'

Jonah drew up from his dream.

'You slide into sleep
    with slaughter in the wind.'

Jonah drew up from his dream:

Out too far
you try to yell
your nose bleeds water.
A girl on the far shore
rubs herself lovingly with lotion
circling and circling
into the dark crescent of hair and
finally your guttering cry
as she looks beyond
the set to the lights.

His Dive

He could have thrown himself over
   board off the stern
at least lost himself in a howl
   allowed the storm to topple
   him, an accident, but
teetering on that edge of oak
   he begged.
The hands of the seamen held to their lines
   firm as superstition
   until it frightened
them & they cast him out
   like their own eye.

He slaps the water flat
   as a whale's fluke.
The sting spreads like fingers
   over his belly
   pulls at his navel.
All around him eels
undulate & glisten like entrails.
He begins to swallow sea
   sucking him
   into its sack.
The bright ribbons stop their quaver
   flash back fixed.
He believes he is peering out
   at his own ribs.

His Song

In the blackness of darkness
he raises an arm & a hand
    as if they were memories.

Drawing knees to his chest
he lies on the floor of the fish
    an insomniac.

The walls are familiar.
It is his mother's room where
    blackness was alive

warm as the breath of a bull
    and he makes her a song:

    Thrown on the ocean
    Into the eye of the sea
The waters of earth surround me.

    Thrown from your sight
    I look toward you.

The waves lay siege
    Close above me.
Sea-weed coils around my head.

    At the base of mountains
    Earth embraces me forever.
You turn your face & lift me up.

His Fear

The never-getting-out-fear
    feeds at Jonah's side
    like the spongy placenta
an always hovering fish, our fear.

    We floated three
    triple-moon turns
in the belly of the mother.
    We rippled gills
    then turned to bone
gathered our brain into a planet
    and turned away
from those traitorous arches
clenching & unclenching us.

    Who was drowned
    yet never got wet
swallowed but not eaten?

A storm of convulsions
slinging through the body
    a glaze of light
at the end of the alley

and Jonah named the light
        God
gave Death indigestion who
    after three days
    threw him up

an exile in our country
where words are mortared into walls
    closets threaten the child
        solitary
    the final punishment.

His Faint

Rain surrounds their house.
His daughter stands in the hall
as if she were the first swimmer.

    Her dripping clothes
    stain the carpet
and Jonah snaps her joy
       like a twig
his fire feeding on itself.
She's consumed in a crackling of words
    that turns on him
    until she cries.

He wants to run the scene
    backwards catching
those flames in his mouth

        but leaves her
    in solitude standing
as if he dreamed himself & her
    and only watched
his mouth a locked cupboard
the intruder's knife moving
    closer & closer
until he can feel its coolness.

Jonah considers suicide
    frightened of what withers
of words that fly
    and do not.

His right hand folds napkins
    sets the table
    and files her nails
aware that his left
contradicts the Master
    seizes a word
    and runs outside
loosing it in the storm like a bird.

His Anger

East of that city as wide
      as three days
      Jonah sulks in the heat—
'God, 60,000 people spared
      the fall-out
for not knowing the right
hand from the left.'

Quail whistle on the hills
      mock
the times his song sang itself
      when words fit
      into place like ribs.

There's a fish, Jonah's thinking
      within us
hears the ocean's retreating
      roar of laughter

or we live in that Leviathan
      traveling somewhere
      we don't know
who's annoyed at the song
prying into her ribs
      like a blues-harp.

Jonah the prophet
his word preying on people
      in the streets
      hardens his arteries
and sits above the city
      picking God
      out of his hair
      cracking him under his nail
      like a flea.

INVENTIONS OF LAZARUS

The Lizard

The Vision

The Clawed Beast

The Lizard

A lizard motionless on the street
    in front of your house
    like a leather tongue.

      Lazarus
    if you had come mute
      or raving, yes
but this damned silence
    full of talk
and your arrogant gaze
penetrating all bodies
    even stone
until their particles flee
      by what right?

You walk the street the old way
    first one foot
    then the other
joke with the children as before.
    Yet again and again
    that sliver of memory how
my mother's death is not mine
how it is more than mine.

At supper I see the bread
breaking down in my body
    obsessed
with rearrangements of itself.

A fly sits wringing its limbs
in some insistent, futile mime.
    I name him 'Lazarus'
    then crush him.
    A cry so small
only grains of stone turn.

    Your light goes out.
    You sleep. You sleep.
What is this death more than mine?
    What is this death?
    In the street the
ponderous reptile silence writhes.

The Vision

Must I tell you again what
  you know?

Despite my will
  that seemed a bone
my body slumped utterly limp
  like a stoned hare.

You expect a story
  and I have none
  returned
to mock you people with my
revelation of the obvious.

Surprised by night
lying in the pits of my skull
  like two stones
  the neck swells
limbs flex into my body what
is more natural than death?

My belly turns pale, blood
dragged into my buttocks
and all of us heard a voice
  christen me Death.

Then you go your own way
  carrying the name
the small dryness in your pockets.

So this is the end, you say
  but the stones did not
    cry
out the lust of the flesh
  remains.

Listen.
  Do you hear feet
  in the acacia tops?
Did you expect
  I would stare
with black-ringed pupils
turn my pockets out?

The buzz and murmur
of my inhabited body
    cease
and my bones appear, dry, solid.

But you know this
I've been accosted by
    bone
been changed
my long habit of living broken.

O lovely whims of those peoples
    who decorate their
    bodies with bone.

The Clawed Beast

He made himself up
in the darkness not
like a mortician pretends but
the way an actor uses light.

And as in a dream
he died
peering at himself.

He was ready to share
with stone its oblivion
to sink for years into silt
memory floating
overhead like hair.

But in his room in that rock
in a fever of solitude
he invented an animal
who made its head blunt
and battered through stone.

With desire curved like claws
it swam upward
against the current of decay.

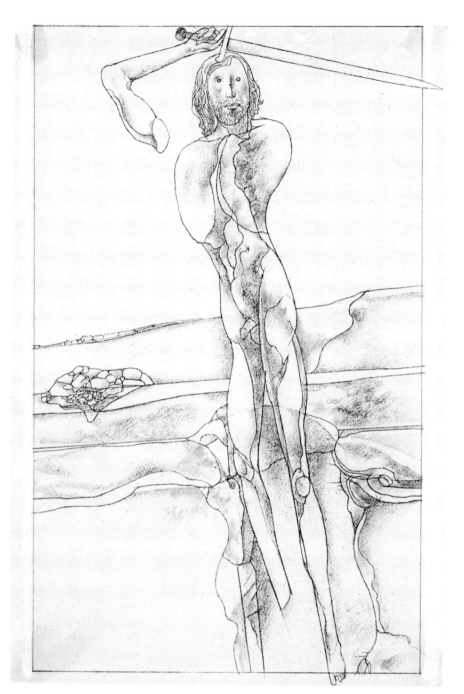

SAVING THE APPEARANCES

Mary Magdalene in the Garden

The Fish Sermon

Five Hundred Witness

Tall Walking Figure

What Thomas Said

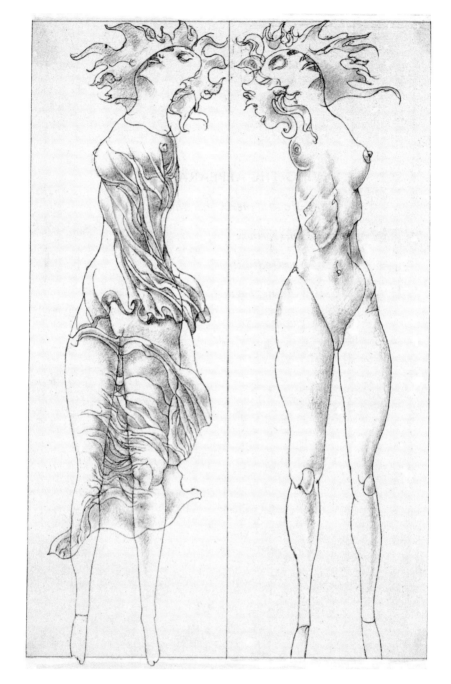

Mary Magdalene in the Garden

Some dawns
    when light seeps
    beneath the edge of dark

    spreading its bright stain

        over the earth

some dawns, I say
    I too
have her Desire
    her whole body full of touch.

I can see her yearn
    through my garden for that old
young garden of Eden
    as though she heard
me call her name.

But I falter at my garden's edge
    as if I had forgotten
my own name.

My step lamed
like seven Doubts deviled Mary.
    Their dirt blind snouts
probed the filaments of her nerves
    clogged her brain.

First, she saw her mother's white hair
    against her own crow-sheen curls
    and knew she was a changeling
    abandoned on the threshold

Later she thought 'maybe father is right
    I am only a reed
    of a girl, not like a boy'

Third, she refused to answer to
    Mary   Mary   Mary

Through the din of her loom
    tin kola, kola, pon pon
    her brother's cry from the cradle,
    but as she seized her shuttle
    silence frayed on the air

Feeling her body slowly ravel
        she wondered, fifth, whether that girl
        in her mirror mocked

Then she asked over and over
        if she is the neighbor's laughter
        if their body is a foreign country
        if her fingers can let in people

                as her accusers tightened around
                in her dream appeared a man
                and as they raised their stones
                he loosed her name
                until each rock grew larger
                split like a chrysalis
                and flowered with wings

And seven, she wondered alone aloud
        in her mind her mother's embrace
        a curve like a moon
        between their bodies,
        whether her small hollow of flesh
        still cups her mother's echoing swell.

Dark plunged like a curtain
to the bottom of her brain

and she drooled in the street
        shocked the crowds
with uncanny thunder
        out of so thin a reed.

Her eyes bolted in their sockets.

Mary met him next in the street.
        He called to her doubts
        disperse
        but their gnawing was loud

        the din jamming Desire

but sudden one climbs to one side
        lets in an ooze of sun
and two climbs down on that side
        stiffens her nipples
and three slides between these two
        into slippery clefts

38

four crowns herself with peacock eyes
five comes forth in many-colored flesh
six enters into one like a seed
and seven agitates herself into a lily
    contains all of Mary.

A reedy quaver of melody
    moves leaves
and the cypress pours its fragrance
    into her body.

And Mary rolled her sweet name
in her mouth as she saw him die.

Just as I tongued mine
    behind the teeth
as my mother was settled in the garden

    O dear father
alone with your desire
    you still rise out of a dream
see her at the foot of your bed
        her tread creaking the floor
        where it ticked at her step
        every night for twenty years
and you answer her as she
    distinctly repeats your name.

I see Mary in my garden
    searching for the man.

    A friend kissed him here
    one eye open
    and he was murdered.

Against the stone wall she vows
    to kiss him with both eyes.

Her yearning perfects the lilies.
    She believes
    her hands are butterflies.

    A stranger approaches.

She recognizes the iridescence of lark-song.

    The gardener speaks her name

and she knows
whose tongue
has touched it.

He refuses her embrace

but as dawn bleeds in the dew
she carries her whole name
full of herself to his friends

and myself with our doubts.

The Fish Sermon

All night cold drizzle
    rots their flesh
ebbing in and out of cramped dreams.
Seven of them on Tiberias
    faces scaled with salt
and now an early morning mist
    hangs in the sun
    like an empty net.

This I imagined.   Yes
    I admit
    they were not my legs
    knotted in that boat.

Yet nothing.
And with the rising of the day
    still nothing.

I am not the one to make this.

And with it mark
    you their hunger.

Hunger screams in their muscles
    like a gull. Throats
constrict in the sodden hemp-smell.
Limp ropes slap the boat's side.
    They turn finally
    toward shore
despair sloshing the gunnels

only to see sand waver with the sea
    land breathing
with their own ebb and heave.
To see a stranger move
slowly along that eel line of shore
    neither earth nor water
but threshold of sand sucking sea
    and sea the sand.

He stands.
Through bright mist they see him
    ripple his skin into scales.
They flick like scavenger fish
    swath him in a scarf of daggers
    tear gobbets of flesh

43

but he stands.

Again
I made this last
    out of my own hunger

but if you will
    it is no dream

        in this
    I was with them
eight of us heard
    the same voice
    swore it floated from shore

    the stranger's.

A sermon, yes, but also song.

Stiff in the mountains
    after a forty-day fast
he came down ravenous
    like us.
He followed the undulant shore alone
    scooped a single fish
devoured part of its body
    and kindled his fire
with the other.
    He flung back
its fragile ladder of bones
    with a sweep of his arm
as if they were to be
    reclothed with flesh.

But I tell you that voice.

We heard his murmur at the fish.
    First
this gentle cajolery
    in a constant whisper
rising and falling
    like a tide
entreating them to come into the net
    without fear
to come and be caught.
    He courted them like a lover
crooning: 'You fish, you fish
    you are all kings

44

in suits of lights'

and the sea swells
as they rise up in a foam.
Some dance along the shore
and he continues like a messenger:
'Come my beauties
you who flash the night into itself.'

Would I had made this song

but I heard it from a salmon-eater
as a boy in California
whose grandfather waking one morning
beside the Pacific
received it whole
from a stranger.

But his sermon was not finished.

And we were confused.
We heard a voice
as real as a dream
certainly, the stranger's
from shore

yet he moved in a sinuous kingdom
we have not visited
where water washed itself into earth
earth into water

though we had glimpsed pieces
fouling out nets:
those leafy sea animals
kelp with eye-tipped stalks

and below us the oozing fish
turning themselves to stone.

We could not escape his voice
even had we wanted.
It forced its music
into our bodies

till that music became our own voice.

Dreams billowed out in our windy heads

like butterfly nets
and we entered that kingdom
of ourselves where

Mental Things alone are Real

this Oar

our Boat as real as the sea

I said, to step is to
tread a swarm of fish.

One knocks my foot boosts
me before I fall lifted
on their glittering backs.
The wave swells me
this undulant field of fish
these beauties our kingdom . . .

but his sermon continued
through the mist
unshriveling our bodies.

He told us to change sides
cast our nets
seven times over a new side
into new water
stretching our limbs to the fish.

At once the nets shred our hands
groaned and writhed
just below the water's surface
like a swarm.
We lost half
and a winter's work of rope
but our hunger
changed.

We broke fish
and our fast
with him on the shore
later told our friends
who were incredulous
yet recognized our tale

for I come back to tell you all

I admit
a hard story.

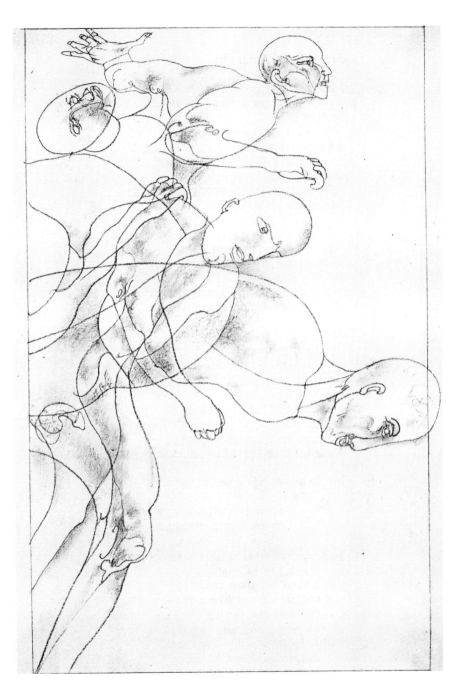

Five Hundred Witness

I am old
    every month open the dead-
bolt lock
    in a rhythm of clicks
take tentative steps on the stairs.
    A blast of sun at the stoop
and I am wary
    crossing the concrete waste
where alleys wait.

    Fourth year
    again by Election
in our land a new Messiah

and a dance to the street chant:
'There ain't no flies on Jesus.'

We are all of us zealots
    the five hundred
    discover in ourselves
a son of man bruised.
We drag our limbs
    into the hills believing

    but some of us wander.
We are those for whom mail arrives

in towns we have never been.

    Throughout the kingdom
    few receive a message.

The hobbed heel splinters his bones
    but a son of man
    knows his own shape.
His tongue moves like a plow
    furrows the brains
    of five hundred, frenzied
within with destiny. He mocks
    deceitful riches
    and Rome itself—
    'You have heard
        Caesar is Messiah
but I say find his silver tax
    in the fish's mouth.'

He speaks a promise:

    'I have not come to bring peace
but a sword'

    and we know the Kingdom
is among us flexed
    in our sleepless bowels
on that hill from where we sweep
    down with a snarl
    the certainty of wolves.

I am young
        and the spores
of mushroom clouds

    flower under my skin.

This the pillar of cloud
    that leads out of the waste?

All of us wanderers finding within

    that we do not
        know what we want
    perhaps do not want
what we know and want
    what we do not know

    always

it has been so.

So many long marches
    and still
Pharoh does not fall away like a scab.

From head full of fear's fever
    Messiah.
From consuming dance on the sand
    Messiah.

Perhaps we do not want
    what we know and want . . .

You have heard
    that the Fuhrer seized our juglar
but I say

he was Elect
by the people
No doubt you have heard also
he was the Devil
but I say he was not malformed
not born with one testicle
was neither celibate
nor sexually deviant
nor were his daydreams bizarre
He was physically fastidious and bashful
yet adventurous
sentimental
efficient
and a good comrade
For a short time he ate too much
but he liked Spaniels
and drew with charcoal.

Like ours
his mother died of cancer.

Fact as if facts could be true.

The Sign: a bent-armed
cross whirls counter-
wise a wheel of knives.

His shape among us neither.

He promises safe streets and bread.

I am old
carry the End in my flesh
stalked from the bank
by sons-of-bitches who cash in
my Social
Security.

I know

sons-of-men

in that kingdom beyond my walls
where letters do not lie uncollected
on deserted stairs

and their dance in the streets:
'There ain't no flies on Jesus'

I am young
    stamp out five hundred steel End-
Yoke a day for GM
    the din
crushes their cry on the street.
    I know
and do not know what I want . . .

His words pulse in the hills:
    'The Kingdom is a man
who wants to assassinate Caesar.
He draws his sword in his house
    thrusts it into the wall
    in order to know
whether his hand will carry through.'

One of us old men escapes
    the gas chamber
        Wilna, Poland

lives in a Jewish graveyard
hidden in a grave.

Nearby a young woman gives birth
    in a grave to a boy
and with arthritic hands
    I coax him out.

As the new child utters his first cry
    I, an old one wrapped
        in a linen shroud
    shout into the sky:

'Who else than the Messiah himself

    can be born in a grave?'

And we five hundred
        see the son of man appear
    though some are fallen asleep.

    Three days later
that new-born child
        sucks dry breasts.

    And we old men read letters
dream dreams

53

and we young in visions
see the chosen dancer
beckon us
with our arm like a tongue.

Tall Walking Figure

The two in twilight, Cleo
   and Cleo's friend.

You cannot see history—
   the Hanged Man.

      His body flickers
      back of their eyes
      on the skull-screen
But their naked feet are clear

      in the foreground
      tacking edge to edge
that road from the city of sentence
   home to Emmaus.

Before them an ocean of desert.
      Villages near sleep.
      The Rebel dead on the Tree
         disappeared.
         Rome alive still.
      Yesterday
beats in their heads.

They move in this metamorphosis
      of day to night
      from one story
to another. Their raised arms
      against the horizon
      accuse each other.

In the twist of their faces
      storm of skin
where a new story churns
         in a froth of forms.
Knowledge explores
      their face like fever

since blood on the tongue
      turned vinegar
      their purpose to water.
      Now another story
an hypothetical cosmos

         its mouth
      of stars opening

over them slowly.

In the curve
        of their mouths
vulnerable as that moon-shell
on the dusk-shifting beach
        above them
you can see their new track—
        to give up
        at catastrophe's edge
like a sailor
        beating close
        to the wind-eye

        to give up
        subduing
for sake of their own seduction.

In the half-light
        their physiognomy
contorted to a NO
        to the tense sentence
        at the story's End. NO
        to the tale that flicks
        like a scorpion's moon-sliver
divides the face with pain.

Those two trudge
        in this scene
        out of the dead
story. They have seen
        its body ride
        the mast-tree
tugging at them to a dead center.

They tack against that inwashing

        centripetal rim

of its maelstrom.

There is no road to Emmaus
        but by sea-change.
A dead body possible
        but not interesting.
They are past blaming
        one another now

yet the friend fears what is
        is not obliged
        to have interest.
Cleo insists that history
cannot avoid the obligation.

On the sea they know this
        that they can know
only by slant.
        History is crooked.
Bearings a scatter

        of the stars'

        Appearances

the scatter that marks
        out a field
of what they do not know
        the ghost
they follow to imagined shores
        characters in a story
of their own telling and when

        LOST

'It is required . . .

        Perdita. Perdita.

'you do awake . . .

        Perdita.

'awake your faith.'

You can see in their eyes
        it is not the stars
as stones or firey whirlpools
        that matter
but the palpable story.

Their eyes turn
        in the half-dark
away from the Hanged Man

that surges over their path
        a sea

sucking at them but

CLEO'S HEAD FLOATS.

Its mouth-cup like a conch
        full of voice—

'They only are protected
        from appearances
who are ruled
    by purpose.'

We see Cleo
exposed in this desert scene.
The Tree's own story
    can bend into him
root in his pathless brain
    where there are no
molecules of will left

    only waves
their flotsam strewn over the sand
    whose grains
reveal where the waves'
    body is not.

The two friends
    with
a third figure.

Cleo blurts his
    story of him hanged
on that windy Tree
    wounded by a spear
himself to himself
    on the skull-hill

and their near drowning
    in disappointment
    the last days

but speaks with eyes aslant
    as if the stranger
    sudden as jetsam
walked in a wave's shadow.

And the crumpled words

inside a beached bottle

are in his own hand—

'You must be chosen

    as witnesses.'

The tall
walking figure
    beside them appears
to know these chosen.
Day whirls
into night. They are flung
    toward Emmaus

by great centrifugal outwashing
    of the axle-tree

    as the stranger
shares with them his bread

    and they know
the Hanged Man manifest
        in another story

    as he opens his mouth:
'Split the tree
    there you will see me'

    as they peer
straight out at him knowing
    that knowledge
    changes the known
        he disappears.

What Thomas Said

      lay in the ear

like laughter

      startled our bodies
out of a lover's tangle.

      As if

      we feared a long guffaw

the hand of laughter

      in our bed.

      As if
aware it was a weapon

      severing private order
        as if

he were the mocking-bird

      of make-believe

that threat again
      we knew as children
to our game's gravest moment

      when the scream exploded
      at those companions:

      "It's not funny

It's not funny."

      His two-edged voice
entered with a blade of light
through the barely open door:

      "If I tell you the words
He said to me
      as I put on a new body
you will take up stones
      to throw and fire
will come from the stones

and burn you up."

The urgency of fire.
    Never before
from our skeptic friend Thomas.
    Or such gall.

His insistent fist on the door.
We wove and unwove
    sudden
as he played
    such effrontery
his voice pacing laughter's edge:

"About midnight I see the sun
    brightly, for midnight
    too is noon.

There is nothing in the room
    without sound or scent
nothing without intonation of color
    lily and canary yellows
    exploding themselves
    in my diamond body.
No difference between the table
    and its bath of light.

Such a play of passions
    over my skin
like oil prisming on water
    where I refract
    in that wave where
    red becomes orange.

My heart out of its cage
    beats above my head
    a great hovering bird

and mother rises up
    wades in the light
    just beyond reach.

    Her face is calm.
One hand beckons.

    She moves as a figure
    across my ground
until I am alone with only

63

the beating in my ears
   a single character
   left on her stage
full of fear that this flapping
of equivocal worlds is forever.

Thought comes in at my nostrils
   like wings of birds
   warping in the wind
until that thrust of my hand

   the telling gesture
   as in some last game
where knowledge and laughter
   confound themselves
together in a sleight of hand.

   I put on a body
   like a cock plunges
its head into the dawn sun
   until I shudder
   seeds of light
   let in laughter
that convulses the room.

The end of the table swells
rises up toward me.
   From the hearth
   flames like branches
begin opening out
   and closing in
opening and coming together
like someone who is happy
   and goes with his hands.

   Corpuscles of light
fill the room with red mist

and the burden of that Man's song
   falls out of a black sun
   beyond the windows—

'My mother never knew me
   my father he buchered me
my sister, little Mak Marie
   she gathered up
   the bones of me
tied them in a silken cloth

64

to lay under the Tree
Tweet,   Twee
what a pretty bird am I.'

I see that bright mystery
the player outdistancing the game
no longer afraid
of the mock chant
and I cannot sleep
for I am changed."

We knew Thomas the Doubter.
Everyone knows
there are no
credulous stone-masons.

He made up this game
as we made move and countermove
and believed
in our own passions

until his body in the door
laughing all light
exploded in us
what we knew.

As if

he had become father

and mother of himself.

He startled our playing
into its make-believe
and our hands fluttered
out of themselves like larks.

His mockery understood
its own play
the dangerous ludicrous.

Like that smartass kid's
crack
broke the grip
of the playground bully
on his own fist.

Thomas told the Man's joke:

"Show me the stone
the builders have thrown away;

that's the corner-stone."

He told us that the Devil
is the spirit of gravity—

"I know
because even as I entered
that acorn of light
Andrew left to piss."

In laughter
we leave ourselves.

From the womb we laugh
and out of dead bellies.

He had feared for his crystal body
"for there is no order
laughter cannot shatter"
then knew its wave
pulsing through him

"holds my body together
in a hover of pretense
like the green light
shakes in a linden leaf."

Standing in the door
his body burned as if
it would change us
with a single motion
to the shape of flame.

"Whoever's near to me
is near to the fire"
the Man's word

and His song's refrain
falling into that room
out of the blaze
of night's highest noon:

"O Mary Mak   Mak Mak . . ."

We knew with Thomas

that the Man had entered
through walls
made from stones of light

"All dressed in black
Black Black."

into a circle of passion
that Thomas joined
with his hand like a child

"O Mary Mak   Mak Mak . . ."

and interrupted our playing
in his body of laughter

"All dressed in black
Black Black."

that did not allow us
gravity
as if he remembered the playground
where to slide down
was to fly up
for he stood singing
in our door's beak of light:

"Tweet   Twee
what a pretty bird am I
Tweet   Twee
what a pretty bird."

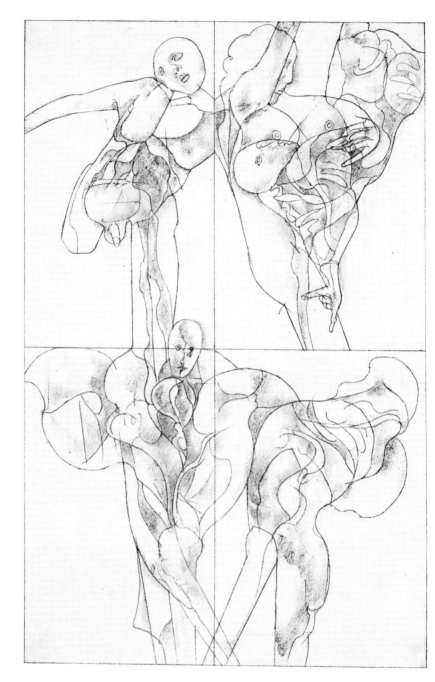

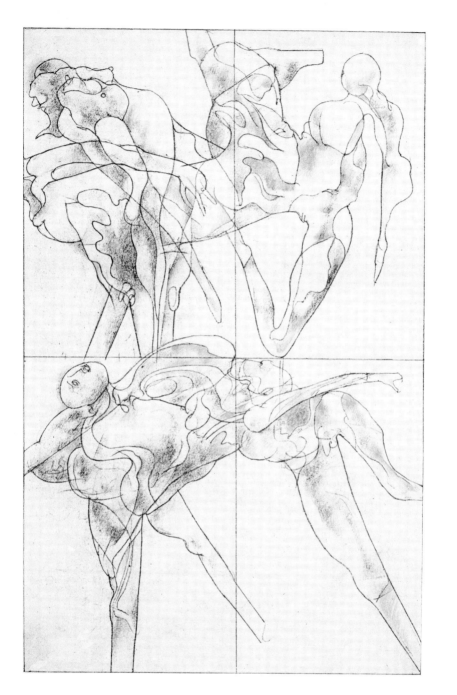

Epilogue

LETTER TO JEREMY, WHO HARPED
THE BLUES AND NOW HOLDS TO GOD

Yes, apparition of your grandfather
          slowly rocking
        rocking
that chill night and gently calling
till you sat like static fur up
watched him drift into mist
          wisps of hair
        disappearing the last moment
          night outside
booming black above the lake

          I believe,
        but on the other hand
          to see God
come across the water
        with his hands
          to say the net
of piney shadows reflects
        God's weather
          or to predict
the sulphur climate of hell
        just in case, casual,
          admits two worlds
        cranking side by side

          damns our single
quivering bedspring of desire
        shot full of quirks
shining beyond all discrimination

        the universe in short
        interpenetrate as trout
this world where we don't know
          which side's dead
        will win the war.

                    #

72

No argument, my friend
  this be testifying blues.
I'm maybe seven
lying in a sack of sweat.
My rows of collected rocks glow
  while fevered phones
  announce themselves
down the tunnels of my ear saying
  I need saving.

And father appears
like a thief in the night
  lifts his hands
  lays them deliberately
  on my forehead
as if the fleshy gifts
  were baseball mitts.

He releases words
over me that hover like hummingbirds.
Only minerals are quiet.
Knots of crystal sulphur
  gleam behind the glass.

God is Here

in this room with his hands
  catching my flames
turning them to cool pyrites.

This is how it is
  when the light changes and
  beside me on the highway
  trailer wheels
  roar like suns the breakneck
  radio blues
  suspending my car
  between divider and rig.
A distant riff of forsythia
  at the eye corner
  and steely string-song
climbs the stratosphere of spring
  frenzied tandems
  rattling my window
and this electric plasma
  holds me
with my hands on the wheel into Jersey and

                    Jesus Christ
        I am a photon of light.

    The ordinary changes my life
        panhandling in the street its
        inexplicable touch
            on the nape-nerve
        like a 5-note lick

        I ain't been nowhere
        I ain't been lost
        I been here all along

    at home with the stranger
        who lights up
        asks a question
    says nothing at my kitchen table
        of the life past death
            has a beer
        and leaves without his name . . .

        In those days Jesus lives
            in the dining room
        a secret brother
    behind the red curtains hanged
        from wrought-iron lances
    and says I am his own whatever else
        to gather at the river.

        When the preacher bends
        me backward into muddy waters
    I can only see the girl

        who just rose up

    scrim of linen clinging to her breasts

        upturned nipples glazed.

    Incandescent, cool particulars
        demand belief
        because it is so hard
    to return through this common
        life to my ordinary
            self

            and all I have—
    Just Am I Am Without One Plea

the hymn seduces
me as it must all of us
creatures of desire.

2 A.M. This is how life
curse the luck the phone beats
into sleep.
Someone's sick or dead. No.
You're gone for good this time.

She sees God again come
across the lake
his arms outstretched.

In the distance between you and me

a lone crow

on the thrumming wire
clutches our conversation with
bone hands.

If it weren't for, weren't for
bad luck my Grandpa the overland king
have no luck at all.
Bobcat blown.
Cave-in at the Catherine.
Every mine a bust
and wanderlust loses Grandma to a preacher
who stays put.

Up the Feather River
moving   moving
the overlander . . .

'love the way my angel spreads her wings'

down with October drizzle
at our door as shaggy
with knowledge as a prophet

Stake'llmakeamillion
prospector blues and shows my hands
to rock a pan on down

blacksand

goldflakes.

Mineral names roar
—mica, garnet, quartz, galena—
drown out mother's announcing
        the Name of God
on him as if words need only be
    pronounced for power:

'The wind bloweth where it listeth
    and thou hearest the sound
            but canst not tell
    whence it cometh or
    whither it goeth
so it is every one born of the spirit'

            so I am born
    of words from his mouth
that believe I understand the assay
        at twelve know
the sly metamorphosis of molecules

as mother's Shakespearean words
        clamor in my ear's pit
        their curious chorus
            embedded like ore.

        How is it this
ingenious improvisor drives

    claimstakes into my hardpan?

        This grand pauper
insistent as weathered rock seeks
        gold in the deep
    invisible folds
invented from outward signs.

His flat map flat on the table.
    I like it like that.
No roads or churches just lines
        nesting
    within lines.

And across the kitchen
        lines brighten
at the window in an agate slice.
The world returns the world to me.
    I like it like that.

76

Passing his hands over the map
like willow-forks witching

    contours shimmer
    and the land's body
    rises between us

    —likeitlikethat—

the smell of lathe oil on his hands
    seducing me to strains
of mother's grieving his explaining:

'If a man has miner's blood in him
he can't never make it on top the ground.
    He's like a mole
    he can tell his way around
    by the kind of rock he's in
but the wind don't make no sense.'

    This is how it ends
with words. Your grandfather
    rocking   rocking
till you wake or the young man,
before the stroke falls like a hawk
        on his heart,
hears a voice—
    'This far, no farther.'

    In the fatness of time
the preacher serves packaged words
    on my mother's body.
The bearers arrive
    refuse to bear
    pushing the steel cart.

    Carrying casual hands
as though they had an extra pair
    they usher the box
    up the aisle
    out the church
    into a crystal of sunlight
    as if it were not there
and they had the right to pass through.

This moment, my friend, I confess
    reveals myself to myself,

sudden clarity from slow
sift,
        as sediments
deposited invisibly
down deep time are pressed to rock,

        that gods
especially the arrogant one

have come to nothing.

They're all dead now

Grandpa underground again and
father folds his tent of bones.
Mother burns with her last desire
—a crematory flash—
then turns to the dark.

I'm left standin' & singin' the
        secular acetylene blues
        how this rock
and roll of ages lies
        in our own at last hands
that in an eyeblink can turn us
        back to light.

        You're right
        no hidin' in that rock
when the sun burn down the
        radio blastin' 'Baby
you're so beautiful you gotta die
some day'

        . . . it's a relief
no miracle but dailiness itself
no universe but the cold-shouldered
        stranger departing
no deposit, no return, no guarantee.

#

As if you pronounced my name
        plain as water
I turn in the dark free
to find my way by the rock I'm in—

Mole Digger   Man I am

78

                    Every Body
          tryin' to find my name

I'madiggermolemanever'bodytryin'tofindmyname

And when I fly through easy

          BLOWIN' D'DIRT

You know I hump hump the ground
          I got a body of dust

Jesus I come

          moving   moving
believing my witnessing
     minute particulars my every
          image even God
     unravels and weaves
our one coat of a world of many colors
          never
     finishing it just

as out of your single blues note

          bending   bending
songs unfold

     like petals.

This is known as
          amazing grace.

          O lead on kindly
     light down the shaft.

     Baptize me like all poets
          by total immersion
     in the earth's body lying
on folded space—O that interstellar
     bedspring of energy.

The windlass clanking us down
     into unfinished lodes,
          the joy
of light following my head's every
          gesture.
Veins of ore branch and leaf.

I see through a mass of quartz darkly
        drifting with the continent
    on seas of molten rock
        and learn to see
    as innumerable hands
burnishing the bronze in a blind-school
        teach us to see
for the first time the sculpture
        we have always seen.

        Singing to the sun

        (damn the phone
        butts into making
        poems and love—
        Hello, it's Grand-
        pa it's for you)

singing the west light changing
        in a stand of oak
singing not because I expect
        the sun to stand still
        but myself to become sun.

        I tramp with strange
        unwelcoming things
greet each one by its own name
        sing the stone walls
between me and the common things

        down

bring new bodies of desire
        into this world
like the kid renames himself,
how remember your name changed

you like Jeremiah who lived
inside his name as if it were
        the body of a howlin' wolf

        JEREMIAH

with the fire in his bones
        dying of his age
blowin' the fuses of the state

that slams him down a shaft

abandons . . .

        bones kindle
keep the hands warm

    Don't cry for the dead
      no blues for the buried
    moan for one gone away instead

again those lamentation blues
witnessin'   singin'   shoutin'

      So let's call
this shouting down
    everyday indifference
Faith, long-lean-legged and
    ain't had nothin' to eat—
the one substance of things desired
    outcrop of the invisible

    she promises nothing

and Grace the summoning of feeling
    by a swatch of weathered
    ordinary copper gutter

gift visible through drab woods
      its edible green
below the suspense of winter sky
    a washed and mottled
malachite not quite but akin to feeling

    as it gathers by chance
      my allegiance
under a sky that holds itself
    in grey readiness, the cold

    a balanced boulder.

Say not what saves but will suffice.

       #

Now how the morning throngs and
    in joy of my desiring,

81

the boy forever interrupting the man
        at his kitchen table
    writing this letter,
sunlight hard in the lane—Ah, Jeremy

to see the fog burn off
            this galena-bright
        glad day

to be alive in this time, Lawd, Lawd,
            to inherit
in the chance of here and now pure
        extravagant privilege

            in our age
to know the gods have simply
        not panned out.

Light darts the narrow shaft.
    My hand
gropes his at the face of the vein
        and I take over rocking
            the hard-rock drill
from my overlander
            underlander Grandpa

who loves the way the angels
        spread their wings and
Ipitit&IpitchityoucanhearmewhenIpant

    Ain't no Kinks in my Tool

    So Hot

    SWEET SHAFT
Iprickit&IlickityoucanhearmewhenIcry
    SWEET HOLE

theMoleman   heBlowby

    YoucanhearmewhenIdie

    YES.

About the Author

Some Biographical Facts as if Facts Could Be True

1) Born in Oakland, David Sten Herrstrom grew up with braceros in northern California working the dusty orchards. . . . 2) Coming east, marrying Constance, fathering a daughter named Tristen, building a house. . . . 3) After earning a doctorate in English literature at New York University, he taught undergraduates for whom he wrote with friends the textbook *Writing as Discovery*. . . . 4) He continues making poems, published in such magazines as *US1, Altadena Review, Nimrod,* and *Berkeley Poets Cooperative.* . . . 5) The results of his struggles to enter into the images of William Blake have appeared in *Blake Quarterly* and the *Bucknell Review.* . . . 6) Westminster Choir College of Princeton, NJ, presented the premiere of his collaboration with the composer Laurie Altman—"A Sonata For J.S. Bach". . . . 7) He once wrote the line: "There is a fire shut in the bones of words". . . . 8) One year he received a Poetry Fellowship from the NJ State Council on the Arts. . . . 9) Working on Wall Street, he imagines ingeniously elegant devices conducting streams of bits over bright strands of optical fiber stretching from Jersey, where he now lives, to California.

About the Artist

Jacob Landau, water-colorist and printmaker, has had over sixty one-man shows, has participated in several hundred group shows, has been the recipient of many awards, including Tiffany, Guggenheim, National Arts Council and Ford Foundation fellowships, and is included in the MOMA, Metropolitan, New Jersey State and Hirshhorn Museum collections among many others. Named Alumnus of the Year by the Philadelphia College of Art in 1985, he has been widely honored as an illustrator, and was represented in "Twenty Years of Award Winners" sponsored by the Society of Illustrators.